Talking Hands

HOLIDAYS AND CELEBRATIONS

DÍAS DE FIESTA Y CELEBRACIONES

WRITTEN BY KATHLEEN PETELINSEK AND E. RUSSELL PRIMM
ILLUSTRATED BY NICHOLE DAY DIGGINS

A SPECIAL THANKS TO OUR ADVISERS: JUNE PRUSAK IS A DEAF THERAPEUTIC RECREATOR WHO
BELIEVES IN THE MOTTO "LIFE IS GOOD," REGARDLESS OF YOUR ABILITY TO HEAR.

CARMINE L. VOZZOLO IS AN EDUCATOR OF CHILDREN WHO ARE DEAF
AND HARD OF HEARING, AS WELL AS THEIR FAMILIES.

The Child's World

Published in the United States of America by The Child's World®
PO Box 326, Chanhassen, MN 55317-0326
800-599-READ
www.childsworld.com

Cover: left, right, back—Comstock Images; frontispiece: left, right—Comstock Images.

Interior 2, 4, 10, 11, 12, 14, 20, 21, 22—Comstock Images; 3, 7, 13, 16, 17, 19, 23—Brand X Pictures; 5, 6, 18—Steve Cole/Photodisc/Getty Images; 8, 9, 15—Corbis.

The Child's World®: Mary Berendes, Publishing Director

Editorial Directions, Inc.: E. Russell Primm, Editorial Director; Katie Marsico, Managing Editor; Judith Shiffer, Associate Editor; Caroline Wood, Editorial Assistant; Javier Millán, Proofreader; Cian Laughlin O'Day, Photo Researcher and Selector

The Design Lab: Kathleen Petelinsek, Art Director; Julia Goozen, Art Production

LIBRARY OF CONGRESS CATALOGING-IN-PUBLICATION DATA
Petelinsek, Kathleen.
  Holidays and celebrations = Días de fiesta y celebraciones / by Kathleen Petelinsek and E. Russell Primm.
    p. cm. — (Talking hands)
  In English and Spanish.
  ISBN 1-59296-453-2 (lib. bdg. : alk. paper)
1. American Sign Language—Juvenile literature. 2. Holidays—Juvenile literature. 3. Festivals—Juvenile literature. I. Title: Días de fiesta y celebraciones. II. Primm, E. Russell, 1958- III. Title.
  HV2476.P4755 2006
  419'.7—dc22   2005027107

NOTE TO PARENTS AND EDUCATORS:

The understanding of any language begins with the acquisition of vocabulary, whether the language is spoken or manual. The books in the Talking Hands series provide readers, both young and old, with a first introduction to basic American Sign Language signs. Combining close photo cues and simple, but detailed, line illustration, children and adults alike can begin the process of learning American Sign Language. In addition to the English word and sign for that word, we have included the Spanish word. The addition of the Spanish word is a wonderful way to allow children to see multiple ways (English, Spanish, signed) to say the same word. This is also beneficial for Spanish-speaking families to learn the sign even though they may not know the English word for that object.

Let these books be an introduction to the world of American Sign Language. Most languages have regional dialects and multiple ways of expressing the same thought. This is also true for sign language. We have attempted to use the most common version of the signs for the words in this series. As with any language, the best way to learn is to be taught in person by a frequent user. It is our hope that this series will pique your interest in sign language.

Anniversary/Celebrate
Aniversario/Celebre

1.

Hands make the letter "X" and move out and in at the same time. Repeat.

Las manos hacen la letra "X" y se mueven hacia fuera y adentro al mismo tiempo. Repita.

3

Birthday
Cumpleaños

1.

2.

Move middle finger from chin to chest.

Mueva el dedo medio desde la barbilla hasta el pecho.

4

Party
Fiesta

1.

Hands make the letter "P" and move in and out at the same time.

Las manos hacen la letra "P" y se mueven adentro y hacia fuera al mismo tiempo.

5

Card
Tarjeta

1.

2.

Make the shape of a card with index fingers and thumbs.

Haga la forma de una tarjeta con los dedos índices y los pulgares.

Gift
Regalo

1.

2.

Hands make the letter "X" and move down and away from the body.

Las manos hacen la letra "X" y se mueven abojo y hacia fuera del cuerpo.

Mother's Day
Día de las Madres

1.

2.

3.

dear
Mom
I
Love
You

Father's Day
Día de los Padres

1.

2.

3.

Easter
Pascua

1.

Hands make the letter "E"
and twist at wrist.

Las manos hacen la letra
"E" y tuercen en la muñeca.

10

Halloween
Halloween

1.

2.

Open and close hands to reveal and cover face.

Abra y cierre las manos para revelar y cubrir la cara.

Christmas
Navidad

1.
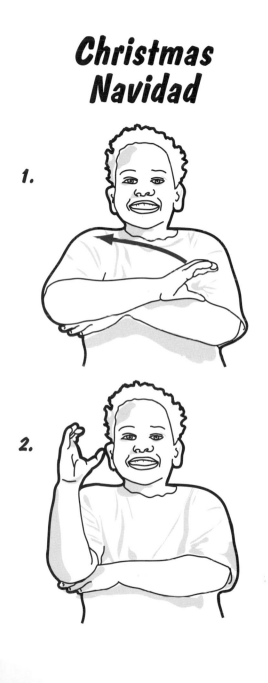

2.

Hanukkah Hanukkah

1.

2.

Move hands outward to show the candles of a menorah.

Mueva las manos hacia fuera para demostrar las velas de un menorah.

13

Thanksgiving
Día de Acción de Gracias

1.

2.

Move hands away from body.
Mueva las manos lejos del cuerpo.

President's Day
Día de los Presidentes

1.

2.

3.

For steps one and two, move hands away from head while closing fingers into a fist.

Para el primer paso y segundo paso, mueve las manos lejos de la cabeza mientras que cierras los dedos en un puño.

Memorial Day
Día de la Recordación

1.

2.

Hand makes the letter "V"and moves from eye towards the side of the head.

La mano hace la letra "V" y se mueve desde el ojo hacia el lado de la cabeza.

New Year
Año Nuevo

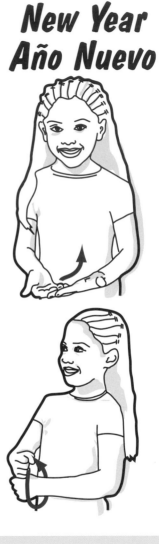

1.

2.

For step one, right hand moves over and up left hand. For step two, right hand moves around left hand.

Para el primer paso, la mano derecha se des liza y se mueve encima de la mano izquierda. Para el segundo paso, la mano derecha se mueve alrededor de la mano izquierda.

Holiday
Día de fiesta

1.

Left and right thumbs alternate between touching the chest and moving outward.

Los pulgares izquierdos y derechos se alternan entre tocando el pecho y moviéndose hacia fuera.

Fireworks
Fuegos artificiales

1.

2.

Open hands as they move outward.

Abre las manos mientras éstas se mueven hacia fuera.

19

Valentine's Day
Día de San Valentín

1.

2.

For step one, make heart shape on chest using middle fingers.

Para el primer paso, haga la forma del corazón en pecho usando los dedos medios.

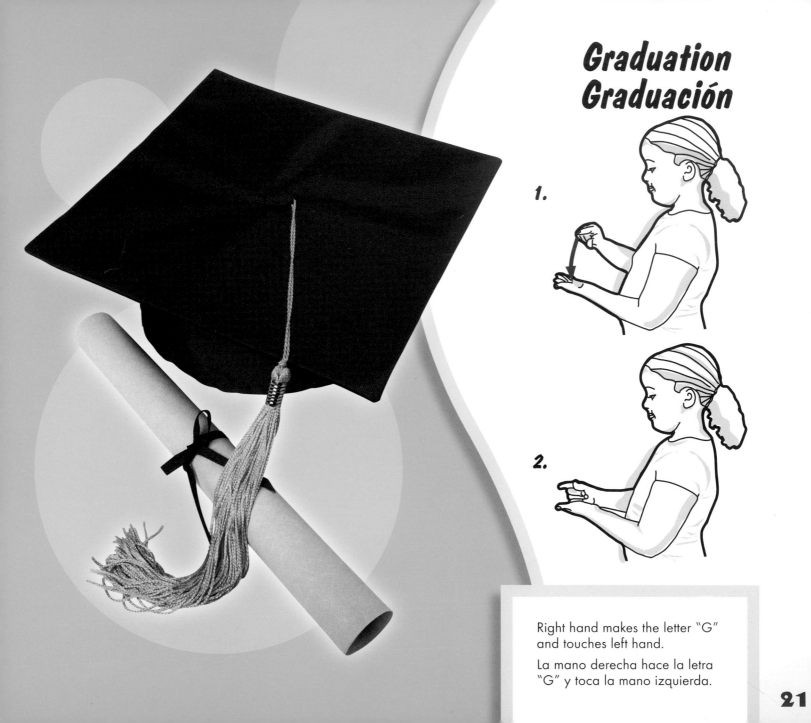

Graduation
Graduación

1.

2.

Right hand makes the letter "G" and touches left hand.

La mano derecha hace la letra "G" y toca la mano izquierda.

Wedding
Boda

1.

2.

Passover
Pascua de los Hebreos

1.

Right fist taps left elbow. Repeat.

El puño derecho golpea ligeramente el codo izquierdo. Repita.

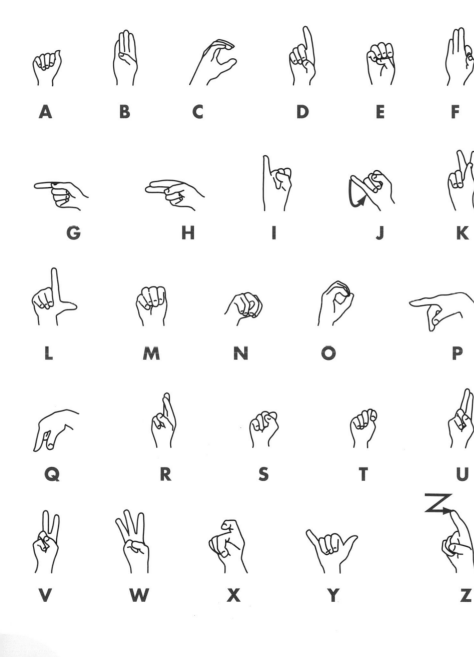

A B C D E F

G H I J K

L M N O P

Q R S T U

V W X Y Z

A SPECIAL THANK-YOU

to our models from the Alexander Graham Bell Elementary School in Chicago, Illinois:

Alina is seven years old and is in the second grade. Her favorite things to do are art, soccer, and swimming. DJ is her brother!

Dareous has seven brothers and sisters. He likes football. His favorite team is the Detroit Lions. He also likes to play with his Gameboy and Playstation.

Darionna is seven and is in the second grade. She has two sisters. She likes the swings and merry-go-round on the playground. She also loves art.

DJ is eight years old and is in the third grade. He loves playing the harmonica and his Gameboy. Alina is his sister!

Jasmine is seven years old and is in the second grade. She likes writing and math in school. She also loves to swim.

P9-DHT-854